TRIVIA QUIZ BOOKLET July 2024 Edition

ISBN: 9798332940804

Imprint: Independently published

Folklore

1- Who was the trickster in Native American folklore?
2- What creature did European folklore describe as fire-breathing?
3- Who is the king of the Greek gods in mythology?

1- Coyote, a cunning and clever character
2- Dragon, a powerful, mythical beast
3- Zeus, ruler of Mount Olympus

4- What did the Japanese folklore spirit Kitsune typically transform into?
5- What is the legendary creature from Scottish folklore?
6- What did Norse mythology's Thor wield as a weapon?

4- Fox, a magical and intelligent creature
5- Loch Ness Monster, a mysterious lake beast
6- Mjolnir, a powerful, enchanted hammer

7- What did the Irish folklore's leprechaun guard?

8- Who is the Aztec god of sun and war?

9- What was the creature in Greek mythology with snakes for hair?

7- Pot of gold, hidden at rainbows' end

8- Huitzilopochtli, a central deity in mythology

9- Medusa, who turned onlookers to stone

English Monarchs

1- What did Henry VIII establish to annul his marriage?

2- What was Queen Elizabeth I's nickname reflecting her unmarried status?

1- Church of England, creating a religious schism and separating from the Catholic Church

2- The Virgin Queen, symbolizing her dedication to England

3- Who succeeded Queen Elizabeth I as the monarch of England?

4- Where did Richard III face defeat, ending the Wars of the Roses?

3- James I, uniting the crowns of England and Scotland

4- Bosworth Field, marking the rise of the Tudors

5- What did King John sign in 1215, limiting royal authority?

6- Who was known as the Merry Monarch during the Restoration?

5- Magna Carta, establishing principles of justice and liberty

6- Charles II, restoring the monarchy after Cromwell's rule

7- What significant battle did William the Conqueror win in 1066?

8- Who was the first monarch from the House of Hanover?

7- Battle of Hastings, initiating Norman rule in England

8- George I, beginning his reign in 1714

9- Who was the longest-reigning British monarch before Queen Elizabeth II?

10- Who was the last Stuart monarch of England?

9- Queen Victoria, overseeing the Victorian era

10- Queen Anne, uniting England and Scotland into Great Britain

Fitness

1- Who is known as the "Father of Modern Bodybuilding"?

2- What did Jack LaLanne pioneer in the 1950s?

1- Eugen Sandow, popularized bodybuilding in the late 19th century

2- Fitness television shows, promoting exercise and health

3- Where did the ancient Greeks develop physical training regimens?
4- Who introduced aerobics in the late 1960s?
5- What was Charles Atlas famous for in the 1920s?

3- Gymnasiums, centers for physical and mental education
4- Dr. Kenneth Cooper, emphasizing cardiovascular.
5- Dynamic tension exercises, promoting strength and fitness

6- Where did Pilates originate in the early 20th century?

7- Who created the first modern fitness club in 1936?

8- What was the main focus of 19th-century Swedish gymnastics?

6- Germany, developed by Joseph Pilates.

7- Vic Tanny, making fitness accessible.

8- Functional movement, promoting health and fitness

9- Who was a major figure in 1980s fitness videos?

10- What did Dr. James Naismith invent to promote physical fitness?

9- Jane Fonda, popularizing home workouts

10- Basketball, creating an indoor sport for exercise

Farming

1- What tool did ancient Egyptians use to irrigate?
2- Who developed the seed drill in 1701 to improve planting efficiency?

1- Shaduf, a hand-operated device for lifting water, was used
2- Jethro Tull, revolutionizing agriculture with precise seed planting

3- What crop rotation system originated in medieval Europe to boost productivity?

4- Where did terrace farming first be a prominent agricultural method?

3- Three-field system, enhancing soil fertility and crop yield

4- Ancient China, effectively managing hilly terrain for cultivation

5- What was a primary crop grown by ancient Mesopotamian farmers?

6- Who invented the mechanical reaper in 1831, revolutionizing grain harvesting?

5- Barley, serving as a staple food and trade commodity

6- Cyrus McCormick, significantly improving harvesting efficiency

7- What innovation did George Washington Carver promote to improve soil health?

8- What was the Enclosure Acts' main purpose in 18th-century Britain?

7- Crop rotation with peanuts, enriching and restoring soil nutrients

8- Consolidating small farms into larger, more efficient agricultural units

9- Where did the domestication of wheat first occur, marking agricultural beginnings?

10- Who introduced crop rotation in 18th-century Britain to enhance productivity?

9- Fertile Crescent, leading to the rise of settled farming communities

10- Charles Townshend, boosting agricultural yields and soil fertility

Endurance Sports

1- Where did the first modern marathon take place in 1896?

2- What is the historical origin of the Ironman Triathlon event?

1- Athens, during the first modern Olympics, honoring the ancient Greek tradition

2- Hawaii, combining three endurance races into one grueling competition

3- Who was the first person to swim the English Channel in 1875?

4- What year did the Boston Marathon first begin?

3- Captain Matthew Webb, completing the swim in 21 hours and 45 minutes

4- 1897, making it the oldest annual marathon in the world

5- Where did the Tour de France bicycle race originate?

6- Who won the first modern Olympic marathon in 1896?

5- France, first held in 1903 to increase newspaper sales

6- Spyridon Louis, a Greek water carrier who became a national hero

7- What distance is covered in a traditional marathon race?

8- When was the Western States Endurance Run first held?

7- 26.2 miles, inspired by the ancient run from Marathon to Athens

8- 1974, evolving from a horse race to a 100-mile footrace

9- Who completed the first recorded 100-mile run in under 24 hours?

10- What is the significance of the Comrades Marathon in South Africa?

9- Gordon Ainsleigh, achieving this feat during the Western States Endurance Run

10- Established in 1921 to honor soldiers who died in World War I

Desert Landscapes

1- Where did the Sahara Desert's ancient rivers once flow?

2- What civilization thrived in the Atacama Desert in ancient times?

1- Across the Sahara, supporting life and creating lush landscapes thousands of years ago

2- The Chinchorro culture, known for mummifying their dead over 7,000 years ago

3- How did the Arabian Desert impact early trade routes?

4- Who first explored the Australian Outback's vast desert regions?

3- It was crossed by ancient caravans, facilitating trade between Asia and Africa

4- European explorers in the 19th century, documenting its harsh and unique environment

5- What major desert did ancient Egypt rely on for protection?

6- Where are the oldest desert paintings found in the world?

5- The Sahara, acting as a natural barrier against invasions

6- Namibia's Namib Desert, with rock art dating back thousands of years

7- How did the Gobi Desert influence the Silk Road?

8- What early civilization developed in the Sonoran Desert?

7- It was a crucial part of the route, requiring traders to navigate its harsh conditions

8- The Hohokam, who built complex irrigation systems in the harsh environment

9- What ancient kingdom existed in the Thar Desert region?

10- Where did early human ancestors survive in desert conditions?

9- The Indus Valley Civilization, known for its advanced urban planning

10- Africa's Kalahari Desert, utilizing its resources for thousands of years

Dreams

1- What did ancient Egyptians believe dreams were messages from?

2- Who wrote the first known dream dictionary in ancient Greece?

1- The gods, providing guidance and warnings about future events.

2- Artemidorus, a Greek diviner who authored "Oneirocritica" in the 2nd century.

3- How did ancient Chinese interpret dreams?

4- What did Mesopotamians use to record their dreams?

3- As omens, reflecting the balance between yin and yang in their lives.

4- Clay tablets, detailing dreams and their interpretations from gods.

5- Where did ancient Romans believe prophetic dreams originated?

6- What did Sigmund Freud consider dreams to be?

5- From the gods, seen as messages about political and personal matters.

6- A window to the unconscious, revealing hidden desires and thoughts.

7- Who in ancient Egypt had the authority to interpret dreams?

8- How did medieval Europeans view dreams about the future?

7- Priests, considered experts in decoding divine messages in dreams.

8- As supernatural signs, often consulted for decisions and predictions.

9- What method did Native American shamans use to interpret dreams?

10- Who believed dreams could predict the outcome of battles in ancient times?

9- Vision quests, seeking spiritual insights and guidance through dreams.

10- Greek and Roman generals, often consulting dream interpreters before wars.

Dragons in Mythology

1- Where did the dragon Fafnir originate in mythology?

2- What dragon did Saint George famously slay?

1- Norse mythology, known for guarding a vast treasure.

2- The Dragon of Silene, symbolizing the triumph of good over evil.

3- Where did the Chinese dragon traditionally symbolize power and strength?

4- Who was the dragon-slaying hero in Greek mythology?

3- In Chinese culture, associated with emperors and control over water.

4- Heracles, who defeated the Hydra as one of his twelve labors.

5- What dragon was defeated by the Babylonian god Marduk?

6- Who rode the dragon Smaug in literature?

5- Tiamat, representing chaos and primordial waters in Babylonian myth.

6- No one, as Smaug is a dragon in "The Hobbit" by J.R.R. Tolkien.

7- Where did the Welsh dragon appear as a national symbol?

8- What did the dragon Nidhogg gnaw on in Norse mythology?

7- On the flag of Wales, representing strength and resilience.

8- The roots of Yggdrasil, the World Tree, in Norse cosmology.

9- Who fought the dragon Ladon in Greek mythology?

10- Where did the dragon Vritra appear in Hindu mythology?

9- Heracles, to obtain the golden apples from the Garden of the Hesperides.

10- As an adversary of Indra, representing drought and chaos.

Digital Art

1- What program did artists use for early digital art in the 1980s?

2- Who is known as the pioneer of digital fractal art?

1- MS Paint, a simple graphic editor included with Microsoft Windows.

2- Benoît Mandelbrot, famous for his work on fractal geometry.

3- Where was the first computer art exhibition held in 1965?

4- Who created the first digital artwork titled "Computer Nude" in 1967?

3- At the Howard Wise Gallery in New York City.

4- Kenneth C. Knowlton and Leon Harmon, using a computer to create the image.

5- What company developed the graphics software Photoshop in 1988?

6- Who was the artist behind the digital work "AARON" in the 1970s?

5- Adobe Systems, which revolutionized digital art and photography.

6- Harold Cohen, who programmed the autonomous art-making software.

7- Where did the term "computer art" first appear in the 1960s?

8- Who used a computer to create digital art for the movie "Tron" in 1982?

7- In the pages of the magazine "Art News."

8- Syd Mead, known for his futuristic design and concept art.

9- What was the primary digital art tool used by David Hockney in the 2000s?

10- Where did the exhibition "Digital Art: Computer Graphics" take place in 1985?

9- The iPad, which he used to create digital paintings.

10- At the IBM Gallery of Science and Art in New York.

Diving

1- What equipment did early divers use to breathe underwater?

2- Who invented the first practical scuba diving equipment?

1- Early divers used a diving bell, an enclosed chamber.

2- Jacques Cousteau and Émile Gagnan, inventors of the Aqua-Lung.

3- Where did the first recorded deep-sea dive take place?

4- What was the purpose of diving suits in the 19th century?

3- In 1930, near Bermuda by William Beebe and Otis Barton.

4- To protect divers from cold water and provide air supply.

5- Who conducted the first successful scuba dive in the 1940s?

6- Where was the first underwater habitat for humans located?

5- Jacques Cousteau, using the Aqua-Lung for underwater exploration.

6- In the Red Sea, known as Conshelf II, built in 1963.

7- What innovation did Hans Hass contribute to diving in the 1940s?

8- When was the first diving mask with a built-in regulator created?

7- The development of the closed-circuit rebreather for deeper dives.

8- In 1957, by Georges Beuchat, enhancing underwater breathing.

9- Who pioneered the use of underwater cameras for marine research?

10- What event marked the beginning of modern recreational scuba diving?

9- Hans Hass, a prominent marine biologist and filmmaker.

10- The release of the Aqua-Lung in 1943, making diving more accessible.

Drummers

1- Who was the drummer for The Beatles?

2- Who was the original drummer for Led Zeppelin?

1- Ringo Starr, renowned for his distinctive drumming style.

2- John Bonham, celebrated for his powerful and influential drumming.

3- Which drummer co-founded The Rolling Stones?

4- Who played drums for The Who?

3- Charlie Watts, known for his steady and consistent drumming.

4- Keith Moon, famous for his wild and energetic drumming style.

5- Which drummer was a member of Cream?

6- Who drummed for the Jimi Hendrix Experience?

5- Ginger Baker, noted for his jazz and rock fusion drumming.

6- Mitch Mitchell, blending jazz elements into his rock drumming.

7- Who was the original drummer for Metallica?

8- Which drummer was part of Nirvana?

9- Who was the drummer for Queen?

7- Lars Ulrich, co-founder and driving force behind the band's sound.

8- Dave Grohl, who later founded Foo Fighters.

9- Roger Taylor, contributing both drumming and vocals.

Dances of the World

1- What dance originated in Argentina and involves close partner connection?

2- Which dance style, popularized in the 1920s, involves quick footwork and lively movements?

1- Tango. It originated in Buenos Aires in the late 19th century.

2- Charleston. It became a popular dance craze during the Roaring Twenties.

3- What traditional Hawaiian dance tells stories through hand and arm movements?

4- Which Spanish dance is known for its rhythmic foot stamping and intricate hand claps?

3- Hula. It is an ancient Hawaiian dance form that uses chant or song.

4- Flamenco. Originating from Andalusia, it combines guitar, singing, and dancing.

5- What is the classical Indian dance form known for its storytelling through expressive gestures?

6- Which dance, originating in Cuba, became popular worldwide in the 1950s?

5- Bharatanatyam. It originated in Tamil Nadu and is one of the oldest dance forms in India.

6- Mambo. It was developed in Cuba and gained international fame through Latin bands.

7- What ballroom dance, known for its rise and fall motion, originated in Austria?

8- Which Brazilian dance is performed during the Carnival and involves energetic, fast-paced steps?

7- Waltz. It evolved in the 18th century and is characterized by its smooth, flowing movements.

8- Samba. It is a lively dance that originated in Brazil for Carnival.

9- What traditional Irish dance is known for its rapid leg and foot movements while keeping the upper body still?

10- Which African-American dance style from the 1930s features acrobatic and swinging moves?

9- Irish step dance. It gained global popularity.

10- Lindy Hop. It originated in Harlem and combines elements of jazz, tap, and breakaway.

Digital Innovations

1- What company developed the first successful personal computer in 1977?

2- Who invented the World Wide Web in 1989?

1- Apple Inc. It launched the Apple II, revolutionizing personal computing.

2- Tim Berners-Lee. He created the first web browser and server.

3- What was the first commercially successful video game released in 1972?

4- Who created the programming language Python in 1991?

3- Pong. Developed by Atari, it was a simple tennis game.

4- Guido van Rossum. Python became popular for its readability and versatility.

5- What was the first widely used search engine launched in 1990?

6- Which digital innovation allowed music sharing in the late 1990s?

5- Archie. It indexed FTP archives, predating modern search engines.

6- Napster. It enabled peer-to-peer file sharing of music files.

7- What was the first social networking site launched in 1997?

8- Who developed the first smartphone in 1992?

7- Six Degrees. It allowed users to create profiles and friend lists.

8- IBM. The Simon Personal Communicator combined a mobile phone and PDA.

9- What was the first web browser launched in 1993?

10- Which company introduced the first e-reader in 1998?

9- Mosaic. It popularized the World Wide Web and graphical user interfaces.

10- NuvoMedia. The Rocket eBook was an early digital reading device.

Dams and Reservoirs

1- Where is the Hoover Dam located in the United States?

2- What is the main purpose of the Aswan High Dam in Egypt?

1- Nevada and Arizona. It provides hydroelectric power and controls floods.

2- It controls Nile flooding. It also provides water storage and hydroelectric power.

3- Which dam created Lake Mead, the largest reservoir in the U.S.?

4- What river does the Three Gorges Dam span in China?

3- Hoover Dam. Lake Mead supplies water to several Southwestern states.

4- Yangtze River. It is the world's largest hydroelectric power station.

5- Which dam is associated with the creation of the Lake Powell reservoir?

6- What is the name of the dam that formed Lake Nasser in Egypt?

5- Glen Canyon Dam. Lake Powell is a major water storage reservoir in the U.S.

6- Aswan High Dam. Lake Nasser is one of the largest man-made lakes.

7- Where is the Itaipu Dam, one of the largest hydroelectric projects?

8- What dam on the Colorado River is upstream from the Hoover Dam?

7- Brazil and Paraguay. It generates a significant portion of both countries' electricity.

8- Glen Canyon Dam. It created Lake Powell and controls water flow to Hoover Dam.

9- Which dam is the largest embankment dam in the United States?

10- What is the primary function of the Grand Coulee Dam in Washington?

9- Oroville Dam. It is located in California and provides water supply and flood control.

10- Hydroelectric power. It is the largest power-producing dam in the U.S.

Diving Spots

1- Where is the Great Blue Hole, a famous diving spot, located?

2- What is the notable feature of the Silfra Fissure diving site?

1- Belize. It is a giant marine sinkhole off the coast of Belize.

2- Between tectonic plates. It is located in Iceland's Thingvellir National Park.

3- Where can you dive with whale sharks at Ningaloo Reef?

4- What is unique about the diving site of Chuuk Lagoon?

3- Australia. The reef is known for its seasonal whale shark visits.

4- Shipwrecks. Located in Micronesia, it is a famous World War II wreck diving site.

5- Where is the Yongala Shipwreck, a renowned diving site, found?

6- What is the main attraction for divers at Blue Corner?

5- Australia. It is a historic shipwreck off the coast of Queensland.

6- Strong currents. Located in Palau, it is famous for its marine life and currents.

7- Where is the famous diving spot of Blue Hole found?

8- What makes the Great Barrier Reef a popular diving destination?

7- Dahab, Egypt. It is a deep sinkhole in the Red Sea.

8- Biodiversity. Located in Australia, it is the world's largest coral reef system.

9- Where is the famous diving location of the Cenotes?

10- What is unique about the diving site at the Rainbow Reef?

9- Mexico. These are natural sinkholes on the Yucatán Peninsula.

10- Soft corals. Located in Fiji, it is known for its vibrant soft coral formations.

Cryptography

1- What was the purpose of the Enigma machine during World War II?

2- Who is considered the father of modern cryptography?

1- German code encryption. It was used to encrypt Nazi military communications.

2- Claude Shannon. He laid the theoretical foundations of cryptography and information theory.

3- What ancient method of encryption involved shifting letters of the alphabet?

4- Where was the Rosetta Stone discovered, aiding in the decryption of Egyptian hieroglyphs?

3- Caesar cipher. Named after Julius Caesar, it involved shifting letters to encode messages.

4- Egypt. It was discovered in 1799 and featured inscriptions in three scripts.

5- Who cracked the Enigma code, significantly aiding the Allied war effort?

6- What is the name of the famous cryptographic artifact from ancient Greece?

5- Alan Turing. His work on deciphering the Enigma code was crucial in WWII.

6- Scytale. It was a tool used by the Spartans for secret communication.

7- What encryption involves using a key to shift letters in the alphabet?

8- Where did the Navajo Code Talkers serve as unbreakable code transmitters?

7- Vigenère cipher. It employs a series of Caesar ciphers based on a keyword.

8- Pacific Theater. They used their native language to transmit secure military messages in WWII.

9- Who developed the RSA algorithm, a foundational public-key cryptosystem?

10- What device was used for secure communication by the Confederate Army during the Civil War?

9- Rivest, Shamir, and Adleman. They introduced the RSA algorithm in 1977.

10- Vigenère cipher. It was adopted for encoding messages during the Civil War.

Digital Marketing

1- What year did Google launch its AdWords advertising platform?

2- Who founded the first recognized email marketing company, Digital Impact?

1- 2000. AdWords revolutionized online advertising with its pay-per-click model.

2- William Park. Digital Impact was established in 1997 and became a major player in email marketing.

3- What platform did Facebook launch for targeted advertising in 2007?

4- What was the first viral YouTube video to reach one million views?

3- Facebook Ads. This platform allowed businesses to target specific demographics with their advertisements.

4- "Lazy Sunday." This SNL skit, uploaded in 2005, became a viral sensation.

5- Who pioneered the concept of inbound marketing in the mid-2000s?

6- What digital marketing tactic did Amazon popularize?

5- HubSpot.popularized inbound marketing.

6- Personalized recommendations. Amazon's system suggested products based on user behavior.

7- When did Twitter introduce Promoted Tweets as a form of advertising?

8- Which company introduced the first clickable banner ad in 1994?

7- 2010. Promoted Tweets allowed businesses to pay for increased visibility on Twitter.

8- AT&T. This ad appeared on HotWired and marked the beginning of online advertising.

9- What digital marketing conference was first held in 2005 by BlogHer?

10- What was the original name of Google Analytics when it launched in 2005?

9- BlogHer Conference. It focused on empowering women bloggers and discussing digital marketing trends.

10- Urchin. Google acquired Urchin Software Corporation and rebranded it as Google Analytics.

Diets and Nutrition

1- What diet did Dr. Robert Atkins popularize in the 1970s?

2- What nutrition plan did Ancel Keys develop in the 1950s?

1- Atkins Diet. It focused on low carbohydrate intake and high protein and fat.

2- Mediterranean Diet. It emphasized fruits, vegetables, olive oil, and fish.

3- What was the primary focus of the Grapefruit Diet in the 1930s?

4- Who introduced the Zone Diet in the 1990s?

3- Eating grapefruit. It claimed to enhance fat burning and aid in weight loss.

4- Dr. Barry Sears. It balanced macronutrients to control insulin levels and inflammation.

5- What diet did Nathan Pritikin create to combat heart disease in the 1950s?

6- When was the South Beach Diet introduced by Dr. Arthur Agatston?

5- Pritikin Diet. It focused on low fat, high fiber, and whole foods.

6- Early 2000s. It focused on good carbs and fats for weight loss.

7- What ancient diet mimics the eating habits of early humans?

8- What diet gained popularity in the 1990s for managing epilepsy in children?

7- Paleo Diet. It includes lean meats, fish, fruits, vegetables, and nuts.

8- Ketogenic Diet. It is high in fat, moderate in protein, and low in carbs.

9- What diet emphasizes plant-based foods and minimal animal products?

10- What diet plan did Weight Watchers introduce in the 1960s?

9- Vegetarian Diet. It includes fruits, vegetables, grains, and legumes, avoiding meat.

10- Points System. It assigns point values to foods to encourage balanced eating.

Don Quixote

1- What is the full title of "Don Quixote"?

2- Who wrote "Don Quixote"?

1- "The Ingenious Gentleman Don Quixote of La Mancha." It was written by Miguel de Cervantes.

2- Miguel de Cervantes. He is considered one of the greatest writers in Spanish literature.

3- When was "Don Quixote" first published?

4- Who is Don Quixote's faithful squire?

3- 1605. The first part of the novel was published in 1605.

4- Sancho Panza. He accompanies Don Quixote on his adventures.

5- What does Don Quixote mistake for giants?

6- Where is Don Quixote from?

5- Windmills. He famously attacks them thinking they are giants.

6- La Mancha. He is a nobleman from the region of La Mancha in Spain.

7- Who is Don Quixote's lady love?

8- What is Don Quixote's real name?

7- Dulcinea del Toboso. She is a peasant woman he imagines as a noble lady.

8- Alonso Quixano. He adopts the name Don Quixote as his knightly alias.

9- How many parts are there in "Don Quixote"?

10- What genre does "Don Quixote" parody?

9- Two. The first part was published in 1605 and the second in 1615.

10- Chivalric romances. It satirizes the popular tales of knight-errantry.

Decorative Arts

1- What style is characterized by intricate floral patterns and curving lines?

2- Where did the Art Nouveau movement originate?

1- Rococo. This 18th-century style is known for its elegant designs.

2- Europe. It emerged in the late 19th century, emphasizing organic forms and flowing lines.

3- What is the primary material used in Japanese lacquerware?

4- Who is a famous designer of Art Deco furniture?

3- Urushi. This natural resin is used to create beautiful, durable coatings on objects.

4- Émile-Jacques Ruhlmann. He was a leading figure in the early 20th-century Art Deco movement.

5- What decorative technique involves inlaying mother-of-pearl into wood or lacquer?

6- Which era is known for its bold geometric patterns and bright colors in ceramics?

5- Nacre inlay. This technique is used to create intricate and shimmering designs.

6- Art Deco. This style from the 1920s and 1930s emphasizes modernity and luxury.

7- What is the term for ancient Egyptian pottery with blue-green glaze?

8- Who is known for pioneering the Arts and Crafts movement?

7- Faience. This material was commonly used for small statues, amulets, and pottery.

8- William Morris. He advocated for handcrafted goods and traditional craftsmanship.

9- What is a famous French porcelain manufacturer established in the 18th century?

10- What decorative art involves cutting and arranging small pieces of glass or stone?

9- Sèvres. This porcelain factory is renowned for its high-quality pieces.

10- Mosaic. This ancient technique creates intricate patterns and images on surfaces.

Dolls and Figures

1- Who created the iconic Barbie doll in 1959?

2- What year was the first G.I. Joe action figure released?

1- Ruth Handler. She co-founded Mattel and designed Barbie to inspire imagination.

2- 1964. Hasbro introduced G.I. Joe, pioneering the action figure market.

3- Which company introduced the first Transformers toys in 1984?

4- What is the name of the famous 1980s He-Man action figure line?

3- Hasbro. The toys could transform from robots to vehicles, becoming a massive hit.

4- Masters of the Universe. This line included He-Man, Skeletor, and other characters.

5- Where did the American Girl doll series originate?

6- Who designed the original Cabbage Patch Kids dolls in 1978?

5- United States. The dolls were created by Pleasant Company in 1986.

6- Xavier Roberts. These dolls became a craze in the 1980s, known for their unique faces.

7- What popular toy line featured small, collectible animal figurines in the 1980s?

8- Which doll line was known for "They're so ugly, they're cute"?

7- Sylvanian Families. These figures depicted various animal families with detailed accessories.

8- Uglydoll. Launched in 2001, these dolls gained a cult following for their unique appearance.

9- What year did the first LEGO minifigures appear?

10- Who produced the first action figures based on the Star Wars movies?

9- 1978. These figures became essential to LEGO sets, enhancing play possibilities.

10- Kenner. The company released the figures in 1978, revolutionizing movie merchandise.

Earthquakes

1- Where did the 1906 earthquake cause massive destruction and fires?

2- What year did the Great Kanto earthquake strike Japan, causing widespread devastation?

1- San Francisco, California. It destroyed over 80% of the city.

2- 1923. It led to the destruction of Tokyo and Yokohama.

3- Which ancient city was devastated by an earthquake in 226 BC?

4- What was the magnitude of the 1960 Valdivia earthquake in Chile?

3- Rhodes. The earthquake toppled the Colossus of Rhodes.

4- 9.5. It is the most powerful earthquake ever recorded.

5- In which year did the Lisbon earthquake occur, severely affecting Portugal?

6- What major earthquake struck San Francisco again in 1989?

5- 1755. It led to fires and a tsunami, devastating Lisbon.

6- Loma Prieta. It caused significant damage and loss of life.

7- Which earthquake caused a deadly tsunami in the Indian Ocean in 2004?

8- What was the primary impact of the 2011 Tohoku earthquake in Japan?

7- Sumatra-Andaman. The tsunami resulted in over 230,000 deaths.

8- Tsunami. It caused massive damage, including a nuclear disaster.

9- Where did the 1995 Kobe earthquake occur, causing severe damage and casualties?

10- What was the death toll of the 1976 Tangshan earthquake in China?

9- Japan. The earthquake led to over 6,000 deaths and extensive damage.

10- Over 240,000. It is one of the deadliest earthquakes in history.

Ecology

1- What did Rachel Carson's book "Silent Spring" address in 1962?

2- Who pioneered the concept of biodiversity in the 1980s?

1- Pesticides' environmental impact. It sparked modern environmental movements.

2- Thomas Lovejoy. He emphasized the variety of life on Earth.

3- Where did the first Earth Day take place in 1970?

4- What was the main focus of the 1987 Brundtland Report?

3- United States. It was a nationwide environmental teach-in.

4- Sustainable development. It highlighted the need for intergenerational equity.

5- Who coined the term "ecology" in 1866?

6- What did the 1972 Stockholm Conference emphasize?

5- Ernst Haeckel. He described the interactions between organisms and their environment.

6- Global environmental cooperation. It led to the formation of UNEP.

7- Where did the first international environmental treaty take place in 1946?

8- What event in 1979 highlighted the dangers of nuclear energy?

7- Washington, D.C. The International Convention for the Regulation of Whaling.

8- Three Mile Island accident. It resulted in a partial reactor meltdown.

9- Who developed the Gaia hypothesis in the 1970s?

10- What did the 1992 Rio Earth Summit address?

9- James Lovelock. He proposed that Earth functions as a self-regulating system.

10- Climate change and biodiversity. It resulted in important environmental agreements.

Endangered Species

1- What species did the Endangered Species Act protect in 1973?

2- Who classified the giant panda as endangered in 1984?

1- Bald Eagle. It helped prevent the species' extinction.

2- IUCN. The population was severely threatened by habitat loss.

3- Where did the last known dodo bird live before extinction?

4- What caused the passenger pigeon to become extinct by 1914?

3- Mauritius. It became extinct in the late 17th century.

4- Overhunting. Excessive hunting led to their rapid decline.

5- Which endangered species did WWF adopt as its logo in 1961?

6- When did the Tasmanian tiger become officially extinct?

5- Giant Panda. It symbolizes conservation efforts worldwide.

6- 1936. The last known individual died in captivity.

7- What conservation efforts helped save the American bison from extinction?

8- Which marine species was declared extinct in 2006?

7- Breeding programs. They increased the population significantly.

8- Baiji dolphin. Habitat destruction and pollution caused its decline.

9- Where did the last Pyrenean ibex die in 2000?

10- What did the IUCN Red List categorize the Javan rhino as in 1965?

9- Spain. Efforts to clone the species have been unsuccessful.

10- Critically Endangered. Poaching and habitat loss threaten its survival.

www.ingramcontent.com/pod-product-compliance
Lightning Source LLC
Chambersburg PA
CBHW070905250726

48662CB00003B/1508